AIR FRYER

Cookbook

The Complete Air Fryer Cookbook Effortless Air Fryer Recipes for Beginners and Advanced Users

TABLE OF CONTENTS

INTRODUCTION

The Air Fryer doesn't come without its stumbling blocks, so here are some essential tips for staying on track as you progress further down the frying road.

- Practice intermittent fasting: Before jumping straight in, steadily reduce your carb intake in the days leading up to your fast days. Short days should be divided into two phases:
- Building phase: The period between your first and last meal.
- Cleaning phase: The time between your last and first meal. To start, try a cleaning step of between 12 and 16 hours and a building phase of between 8 and 12 hours. As your body alters to the change, you will find yourself in a position to tackle a 4-6-hour building time and an 18-20-hour cleaning phase.
- Consume salt: Too much sodium is generally deemed as unhealthy. However, a low-carb diet necessitates a high salt intake, as this type of regimen reduces your insulin levels and flushes out more elevated amounts of sodium from your kidneys. As a result, your sodium/potassium ratio is disrupted. Here are some tips to counteract this change:

- Add a quarter teaspoon of pink salt to every glass of water you drink.
- Incorporate kelp, nori, or dulse into your meals.
- Season your food with generous helpings of pink salt.
- Snack on pumpkin seeds or macadamia nuts.
- Drink organic broth intermittently throughout the day.
- Eat cucumber and celery, both of which contain natural sodium.
- Exercise regularly: Daily rigorous exercise can help activate glucose molecules called GLUT-4, which are needed to return glucose to fat and muscle tissues. Additionally, it can double the amount of protein present in both the liver and the muscles.
- Watch how much protein you eat: Protein is integral to Air Fryer cooking but maintaining a proper balance is necessary. If you eat too various protein-rich foods, you will end up converting the amino acids into glucose (through a process called gluconeogenesis). In the initial stages of your frying, vary the amounts of protein you consume. It is to feel how much is too much.
- Pick your carbs wisely: The few carb-rich foods you do consume should be selected very carefully. It is best to stick to starchy veggies and fruits like berries, apples, lemons, and oranges. For a quick

morning hit, blend them into a healthy green smoothie.

- Take MCT oil: High-quality MCTs are incredibly useful in replenishing the energy levels you deplete throughout the day. MCT oil can be used for cooking, as well as added to beverages like coffee, tea, smoothies, protein shakes, and so on.

- Minimize your stress: Stress is a significant factor in decreased energy levels, so constant pressure may serve as a threat to your cooking success. If you find yourself especially prone to stress at the moment, it may be wise to avoid dieting until you're in a better position to deal with the blow to your energy levels.

- Improve the quality of your sleep: Sleep is essential for managing stress, among other things. Make sure your bedroom is conducive to a good night's rest. It means sleeping in a comfortable bed, in a darkened room, no warmer than 70 degrees. Most adults function best on 7 to 9 hours of sleep every night, though an incredibly stressful lifestyle may require even longer.

- Eat ghee: Ghee works well as a butter substitute, as it can be used in more or less all the same ways and is exponentially healthier. Try frying meat or vegetables in it for a high-fat, healthy meal.

- Seek out Omega 3s: If you find it hard to integrate Omega-3-rich foods into your diet, then you might consider taking supplements. You should make sure your Omega 3 intake matches your Omega 6s. Omega 3 is an extremely beneficial kind of fat, which is crucial to healthy frying.

- Avoid alcohol: It may be hard to kiss the booze goodbye, but it is well-attested that alcohol impedes weight loss. Stay focused on your goals and order a glass of tonic water at the bar instead.
- Drink lemon water: Lemon water is a tasty and refreshing alternative to tap water that has the added benefit of balancing your pH levels.
- Avoid 'sugar-free' products: These labels may sound appealing, but the vast majority of products advertised as 'sugar-free' or 'light' contain more carbs than the original!
- Buy a food scale: Food scales are a great utensil to keep handy in your kitchen as they help you accurately monitor what you are putting into your body. They are indispensable in tracking your carb and overall caloric intake. Invest in your success – get a high-quality, durable scale with a conversion button, automatic shutdown, tare function, and a removable plate.
- Stay carb-savvy: To tackle the inevitable carb cravings, it is a good idea to make yourself aware of the many alternatives that exist. When the urge to order a bucket of fried chicken or a box of pad Thai arises, fight back with these tasty and healthy substitutes:

- Shirataki noodles are made from yams and make a great low-carb alternative to pasta.
- Cauliflower rice, basically shredded cauliflower, mimics the texture and neutral taste of white or brown rice.
- Spaghetti squash can be cut into the shape of noodles with a spiralizer or a fork. It tastes excellent and amounts to less than half the carbs and calories of traditional noodles.
- Heavy whipping cream or almond milk goes great in your coffee instead of regular creamer, which is rich in calories.
- Low-carb bread and tortillas are available for those who can't seem to kick the bread addiction.
- Protein powder can satisfy your sweet tooth in a shake or smoothie. It comes in a wide variety of flavors and is easily incorporated into practically any meal. Plus, needless to say, its high protein content is an added benefit, offering an easy boost to your health.

BREAKFAST

Savory Cheese and Bacon Muffins

Preparation Time: 5 minutes

Cooking Time: 17 minutes

Servings: 4

Ingredients:

- 1 ½ cup of all-purpose flour
- 2 tsps. of baking powder
- ½ cup of milk
- 2 eggs
- 1 tbsp. of freshly chopped parsley
- 4 cooked and chopped bacon slices
- 1 thinly chopped onion
- ½ cup of shredded cheddar cheese
- ½ tsp. of onion powder
- 1 tsp. of salt
- 1 tsp. of black pepper

Directions:

1. Turn on your Air Fryer to 360°F.
2. Using a large bowl, add and stir all the ingredients until it mixes properly.
3. Then grease the muffin cups with a nonstick cooking spray or line it with a parchment paper. Pour the batter proportionally into each muffin cup.
4. Place it inside your Air Fryer and bake it for 15 minutes
5. Thereafter, carefully remove it from your Air Fryer and allow it to chill.
6. Serve and enjoy!

Nutrition: Calories: 180 Fat: 18g Carbs: 16g Protein: 15g

Best Air-Fried English Breakfast

Preparation Time: 5 minutes

Cooking Time: 20 minutes

Servings: 4

Ingredients:
- 8 sausages
- 8 bacon slices
- 4 eggs
- 1 (16-oz.) can have baked beans
- 8 slices of toast

Directions:
1. Add the sausages and bacon slices to your Air Fryer and cook them for 10 minutes at a 320°F.
2. Using a ramekin or heat-safe bowl, add the baked beans, then place another ramekin and add the eggs and whisk.
3. Place it inside your Air Fryer and cook it for an additional 10 minutes or until everything is done.
4. Serve and enjoy!

Nutrition: Calories: 850 Fat: 40g Carbs: 20g Protein: 48g

Sausage and Cream Cheese Biscuits

Preparation Time: 5 minutes

Cooking Time: 15 minutes

Serving: 5

Ingredients:

- 12 oz. chicken breakfast sausage
- 1 (6 oz.) can biscuits
- ⅛ cup cream cheese

Directions:

1. Form the sausage into 5 small patties.
2. Place the sausage patties in the Air Fryer. Cook for 5 minutes a at 360°F
3. Open the Air Fryer. Flip the patties. Cook for an additional 5 minutes
4. Remove the cooked sausages from the Air Fryer.
5. Separate the biscuit dough into 5 biscuits.
6. Place the biscuits in the Air Fryer. Cook for 3 minutes
7. Open the Air Fryer. Flip the biscuits. Cook for an additional 2 minutes
8. Remove the cooked biscuits from the Air Fryer.
9. Split each biscuit in half. Spread 1 tsp. of cream cheese onto the bottom of each biscuit. Top with a sausage patty and the other half of the biscuit, and serve.

Nutrition: Calories: 240 Fat: 13g Carbs: 20g Protein: 9g

Cheesy Tater Tot Breakfast Bake

Preparation Time: 5 minutes
Cooking Time: 20 minutes
Servings: 4

Ingredients:
- 4 eggs
- 1 cup milk
- 1 tsp. onion powder
- Salt
- Pepper
- Cooking oil
- 12 oz. ground chicken sausage
- 1-lb. frozen tater tots
- ¾ cup shredded Cheddar cheese

Directions:
1. In a medium bowl, whisk the eggs. Add the milk, onion powder, and salt and pepper to taste. Stir to combine.
2. Spray a skillet with cooking oil and set over medium-high heat. Add the ground sausage. Using a spatula or spoon, break the sausage into smaller pieces. Cook for 3 to 4 minutes at 360°F, until the sausage is brown. Remove from heat and set aside.
3. Spray a barrel pan with cooking oil. Make sure to cover the bottom and sides of the pan. Place the tater tots in the barrel pan. Cook for 6 minutes

4. Open the Air Fryer and shake the pan, then add the egg mixture and cooked sausage. Cook for an additional 6 minutes. Open the Air Fryer and sprinkle the cheese over the tater tot bake. Cook for an additional 2 to 3 minutes. Cool before serving.

Nutrition: Calories: 518 Fat: 30g Carbs: 31g Protein: 30g

Breakfast Grilled Ham and Cheese

Preparation Time: 5 minutes

Cooking Time: 10 minutes

Servings: 2

Ingredients:

- 1 tsp. butter
- 4 slices bread
- 4 slices smoked country ham
- 4 slices Cheddar cheese
- 4 thick slices tomato

Directions:

1. Spread ½ tsp. of butter onto one side of 2 slices of bread. Each sandwich will have 1 slice of bread with butter and 1 slice without.
2. Assemble each sandwich by layering 2 slices of ham, 2 slices of cheese, and 2 slices of tomato on the unbuttered pieces of bread. Top with the other bread slices, buttered side up.
3. Place the sandwiches in the Air Fryer buttered-side down. Cook for 4 minutes at 330°F
4. Open the Air Fryer. Flip the grilled cheese sandwiches. Cook for an additional 4 minutes
5. Cool before serving. Cut each sandwich in half and enjoy.

Nutrition: Calories: 525 Fat: 25g Carbs: 34g Protein: 41g

Classic Hash Browns

Preparation Time: 15 minutes
Cooking Time: 20 minutes
Servings: 4

Ingredients:
- 4 russet potatoes
- 1 tsp. paprika
- Salt
- Pepper
- Cooking oil

Directions:
1. Peel the potatoes using a vegetable peeler. Using a cheese grater shred the potatoes. If your grater has different-size holes, use the area of the tool with the largest holes.
2. Put the shredded potatoes in a large bowl of cold water. Let sit for 5 minutes Cold water helps remove excess starch from the potatoes. Stir to help dissolve the starch.
3. Dry out the potatoes and dry with paper towels or napkins. Make sure the potatoes are completely dry.
4. Season the potatoes with the paprika and salt and pepper to taste.
5. Spray the potatoes with cooking oil and transfer them to the Air Fryer. Cook for 20 minutes at

360°F and shake the basket every 5 minutes (a total of 4 times).

6. Cool before serving.

Nutrition: Calories: 150 Fat: 9g Carbs: 34g Protein: 4g

Canadian Bacon and Cheese English Muffins

Preparation Time: 5 minutes

Cooking Time: 10 minutes

Servings: 4

Ingredients:

- 4 English muffins
- 8 slices Canadian bacon
- 4 slices cheese
- Cooking oil

Directions:

1. Split each English muffin. Assemble the breakfast sandwiches by layering 2 slices of Canadian bacon and 1 slice of cheese onto each English muffin bottom. Put the other half on top of the English muffin. Place the sandwiches in the Air Fryer. Spray the top of each with cooking oil. Cook for 4 minutes at 380°F
2. Open the Air Fryer and flip the sandwiches. Cook for an additional 4 minutes
3. Cool before serving.

Nutrition: Calories: 333 Fat: 14g Carbs: 27g Protein: 24g

Radish Hash Browns

Preparation Time: 10 minutes
Cooking Time: 13 minutes
Servings: 4

Ingredients:

- 1 lb. radishes, washed and cut off roots
- 1 tbsp. olive oil
- 1/2 tsp. paprika
- 1/2 tsp. onion powder
- 1/2 tsp. garlic powder
- 1 medium onion
- 1/4 tsp. pepper
- 3/4 tsp. sea salt

Directions:

1. Slice onion and radishes using a mandolin slicer.
2. Add sliced onion and radishes in a large mixing bowl and toss with olive oil.
3. Transfer onion and radish slices in Air Fryer basket and cook at 360°F for 8 minutes Shake basket twice.
4. Return onion and radish slices in a mixing bowl and toss with seasonings.
5. Again, cook onion and radish slices in Air Fryer basket for 5 minutes at 400°F. Shake the basket halfway through.
6. Serve and enjoy.

Nutrition: Calories: 62 Fat: 3.7g Carbs: 7.1g Protein: 1.2g

Vegetable Egg Cups

Preparation Time: 10 minutes

Cooking Time: 20 minutes

Servings: 4

Ingredients:

- 4 eggs
- 1 tbsp. cilantro, chopped
- 4 tbsp. half and half
- 1 cup cheddar cheese, shredded
- 1 cup vegetables, diced
- Pepper
- Salt

Directions:

1. Sprinkle four ramekins with cooking spray and set aside.
2. In a mixing bowl, whisk eggs with cilantro, half and half, vegetables, 1/2 cup cheese, pepper, and salt.
3. Pour egg mixture into the four ramekins.
4. Place ramekins in Air Fryer basket and cook at 300°F for 12 minutes
5. Top with remaining 1/2 cup cheese and cook for 2 minutes more at 400°F.
6. Serve and enjoy.

Nutrition: Calories: 194 Fat: 11.5g Carbs: 6g Protein: 13g

Spinach Frittata

Preparation Time: 5 minutes
Cooking Time: 8 minutes
Servings: 1

Ingredients:

- 3 eggs
- 1 cup spinach, chopped
- 1 small onion, minced
- 2 tbsp. mozzarella cheese, grated
- Pepper
- Salt

Directions:

1. Preheat the Air Fryer to 350°F. Spray Air Fryer pan with cooking spray.
2. In a bowl, whisk eggs with remaining ingredients until well combined.
3. Pour egg mixture into the prepared pan and place pan in the Air Fryer basket.
4. Cook frittata for 8 minutes or until set. Serve and enjoy.

Nutrition: Calories: 384 Fat: 23.3g Carbs: 10.7g Protein: 34.3g

LUNCH

Flavorful Steak

Preparation Time: 10 Minutes

Cooking Time: 18 Minutes

Servings: 2

Ingredients:

- Two steaks, rinsed and pat dry
- ½ tsp garlic powder
- 1 tsp olive oil
- Pepper
- Salt

Directions:

1. Scour steaks with olive oil and season with garlic powder, pepper, and salt.
2. Preheat the instant vortex air fryer oven to 400 F.
3. Place steaks on air fryer oven pan and air fry for 10-18 minutes, turning halfway through.
4. Serve and enjoy.

Nutrition: Calories 361 Fat 10.9 g Carbs 0.5 g Protein 61.6 g

Easy Rosemary Lamb Chops

Preparation Time: 10 Minutes
Cooking Time: 6 Minutes
Servings: 4

Ingredients:

- Four lamb chops
- 2 tbsp dried rosemary
- ¼ cup fresh lemon juice
- Pepper
- Salt

Directions:

1. In a small bowl, mix lemon juice, rosemary, pepper, and salt. Brush lemon juice rosemary mixture over lamb chops.
2. Place lamb chops on air fryer oven tray and air fry at 400 F for 3 minutes. Turn lamb chops to the other side and cook for 3 minutes more. Serve and enjoy.

Nutrition: Calories 267 Fat 21.7 g Carbs 1.4 g Protein 16.9 g

BBQ Pork Ribs

Preparation Time: 10 Minutes

Cooking Time: 12 Minutes

Servings: 6

Ingredients:

- One slab baby back pork rib, cut into pieces
- ½ cup BBQ sauce
- ½ tsp paprika
- Salt

Directions:

1. Add pork ribs in a mixing bowl. Add BBQ sauce, paprika, and salt over pork ribs and coat well, and set aside for 30 minutes
2. Preheat the instant vortex air fryer oven to 350 F. Arrange marinated pork ribs on an instant vortex air fryer oven pan and cook for 10-12 minutes. Turn halfway through.
3. Serve and enjoy.

Nutrition: Calories 145 Fat 7 g Carbs 10 g Protein 9 g

Juicy Steak Bites

Preparation Time: 10 Minutes
Cooking Time: 9 Minutes
Servings: 4

Ingredients:

- 1 lb. sirloin steak, cut into bite-size pieces
- 1 tbsp steak seasoning
- 1 tbsp olive oil
- Pepper
- Salt

Directions:

1. Preheat the instant vortex air fryer oven to 390 F.
2. Add steak pieces into the large mixing bowl. Add steak seasoning, oil, pepper, and salt over steak pieces and toss until well coated.
3. Transfer steak pieces on instant vortex air fryer pan and air fry for 5 minutes
4. Turn steak pieces to the other side and cook for 4 minutes more.
5. Serve and enjoy.

Nutrition: Calories 241 Fat 10.6 g Carbs 0 g Protein 34.4 g

Greek Lamb Chops

Preparation Time: 10 Minutes
Cooking Time: 10 Minutes
Servings: 4

Ingredients:

- 2 lbs. lamb chops
- 2 tsp garlic, minced
- 1 ½ tsp dried oregano
- ¼ cup fresh lemon juice
- ¼ cup olive oil

Directions:

1. Add lamb chops in a mixing bowl. Add remaining ingredients over the lamb chops and coat well.
2. Arrange lamb chops on the air fryer oven tray and cook at 400 F for 5 minutes
3. Turn lamb chops and cook for 5 minutes more.
4. Serve and enjoy.

Nutrition: Calories 538 Fat 29.4 g Carbs 1.3 g Protein 64 g

Easy Beef Roast

Preparation Time: 10 Minutes

Cooking Time: 45 Minutes

Servings: 6

Ingredients:

- 2 ½ lbs. beef roast
- 2 tbsp Italian seasoning

Directions:

1. Arrange roast on the rotisserie spite.
2. Rub roast with Italian seasoning, then insert into the instant vortex air fryer oven.
3. Air fry at 350 F for 45 minutes or until the roast's internal temperature reaches 145 F.
4. Slice and serve.

Nutrition: Calories 365 Fat 13.2 g Carbs 0.5 g Protein 57.4 g

Simple Beef Patties

Preparation Time: 10 Minutes
Cooking Time: 13 Minutes
Servings: 4

Ingredients:

- 1 lb. ground beef
- ½ tsp garlic powder
- ¼ tsp onion powder
- Pepper
- Salt

Directions:

1. Preheat the instant vortex air fryer oven to 400 F.
2. Add ground meat, garlic powder, onion powder, pepper, and salt into the mixing bowl and mix until well combined.
3. Make even shape patties from meat mixture and arrange on air fryer pan.
4. Place pan in instant vortex air fryer oven.
5. Cook patties for 10 minutes Turn patties after 5 minutes
6. Serve and enjoy.

Nutrition: Calories 212 Fat 7.1 g Carbs 0.4 g Protein 34.5 g

Marinated Pork Chops

Preparation Time: 10 Minutes
Cooking Time: 30 Minutes
Servings: 2

Ingredients:

- Two pork chops, boneless
- 1 tsp garlic powder
- ½ cup flour
- 1 cup buttermilk
- Pepper

Directions:

1. Add pork chops and buttermilk in a zip-lock bag. Cover bag and place in the refrigerator overnight.
2. In another zip-lock bag, add flour, garlic powder, pepper, and salt.
3. Remove marinated pork chops from buttermilk and add in flour mixture and shake until well coated.
4. Preheat the instant vortex air fryer oven to 380 F.
5. Spray air fryer tray with cooking spray.
6. Arrange pork chops on a tray and air fryer for 28-30 minutes. Turn pork chops after 18 minutes
7. Serve and enjoy.

Nutrition: Calories 424 Fat 21.3 g Carbs 30.8 g Protein 25.5 g

Simple Beef Sirloin Roast

Preparation Time: 10 Minutes
Cooking Time: 50 Minutes
Servings: 8

Ingredients:

- 2½ pounds sirloin roast
- Salt and ground black pepper, as required

Directions:

1. Rub the roast with salt and black pepper generously.
2. Insert the rotisserie rod through the roast.
3. Insert the rotisserie forks, one on each rod's side, to secure the rod to the chicken.
4. Select "Roast" and then adjust the temperature to 350 degrees F.
5. Set the timer for 50 minutes and press the "Start."
6. When the display shows "Add Food," press the red lever down.
7. Weight the left side of the rod into the Vortex.
8. Now, turn the rod's left side into the groove along the metal bar so it will not move.
9. Then, close the door and touch "Rotate." Press the red lever to release the rod when cooking time is complete.
10. Remove from the Vortex.

11.   Place the roast onto a platter for about 10 minutes before slicing.

12.   With a sharp knife, cut the roast into desired sized slices and serve.

Nutrition: Calories 201 Fat 8.8 g Carbs 0 g Protein 28.9 g

Seasoned Beef Roast

Preparation Time: 10 Minutes

Cooking Time: 45 Minutes

Servings: 10

Ingredients:

- 3 pounds beef top roast
- One tablespoon olive oil
- Two tablespoons Montreal steak seasoning

Directions:

1. Coat the roast with oil and then rub with the seasoning generously.
2. With kitchen twines, tie the roast to keep it compact. Arrange the roast onto the cooking tray.
3. Select "Air Fry" and then alter the temperature to 360 degrees F. Set the timer for 45 minutes and press the "Start."
4. If the display shows "Add Food," insert the cooking tray in the center position.
5. When the display shows "Turn Food," do nothing.
6. When cooking time is complete, take away the tray from Vortex.
7. Place the roast onto a platter for about 10 minutes before slicing.
8. With a sharp knife, cut the roast into desired sized slices and serve.

Nutrition: Calories 269 Fat 9.9 g Carbs 0 g Fiber 0 g

DINNER

Breaded Scallops

Preparation time: 5 minutes

Cooking time: 7 minutes

Servings: 4

Ingredients:

- 1 egg
- 3 tablespoons flour
- 1 cup bread crumbs
- 1 pound (454 g) fresh scallops
- 2 tablespoons olive oil
- Salt and black pepper, to taste

Directions:

1. In a bowl, lightly beat the egg. Place the flour and bread crumbs into separate shallow dishes.
2. Dredge the scallops in the flour and shake off any excess. Dip the flour-coated scallops in the beaten egg and roll in the bread crumbs.
3. Brush the scallops generously with olive oil and season with salt and pepper, to taste. Transfer the scallops to the air flow racks.
4. Slide the racks into the air fryer oven. Press the Power Button. Cook at 360ºF (182ºC) for 7 minutes.
5. Flip the scallops halfway through the cooking time.
6. When cooking is complete, the scallops should reach an internal temperature of just 145ºF (63ºC) on a meat thermometer. Remove from the

air fryer oven. Let the scallops cool for 5 minutes and serve.

Nutrition: Calories: 240 Fat: 10 Fiber: 2 Carbs: 24 Protein: 12

Browned Shrimp Patties

Preparation time: 15 minutes

Cooking time: 12 minutes

Servings: 4

Ingredients

- ½ pound (227 g) raw shrimp, shelled, deveined, and chopped finely
- 2 cups cooked sushi rice
- ¼ cup chopped red bell pepper
- ¼ cup chopped celery
- ¼ cup chopped green onion
- 2 teaspoons Worcestershire sauce
- ½ teaspoon salt
- ½ teaspoon garlic powder
- ½ teaspoon Old Bay seasoning
- ½ cup plain bread crumbs
- Cooking spray

Directions:

1. Put all the ingredients except the bread crumbs and oil in a large bowl and stir to incorporate.
2. Scoop out the shrimp mixture and shape into 8 equal-sized patties with your hands, no more than ½-inch thick. Roll the patties in the bread crumbs on a plate and spray both sides with cooking spray. Place the patties in the air flow racks.

3. Slide the racks into the air fryer oven. Press the Power Button. Cook at 390ºF (199ºC) for 12 minutes.
4. Flip the patties halfway through the cooking time.
5. When cooking is complete, the outside should be crispy brown. Remove from the air fryer oven. Divide the patties among four plates and serve warm.

Nutrition: Calories: 240 Fat: 10 Fiber: 2 Carbs: 24 Protein: 12

Butter-Wine Baked Salmon

Preparation time: 5 minutes
Cooking time: 10 minutes
Servings: 4

Ingredients:

- 4 tablespoons butter, melted
- 2 cloves garlic, minced
- Sea salt and ground black pepper, to taste
- ¼ cup dry white wine
- 1 tablespoon lime juice
- 1 teaspoon smoked paprika
- ½ teaspoon onion powder
- 4 salmon steaks
- Cooking spray

Directions:

1. Place all the ingredients except the salmon and oil in a shallow dish and stir to mix well.
2. Add the salmon steaks, turning to coat well on both sides. Transfer the salmon to the refrigerator to marinate for 30 minutes.
3. When ready, put the salmon steaks in the air flow racks, discarding any excess marinade. Spray the salmon steaks with cooking spray.
4. Slide the racks into the air fryer oven. Press the Power Button. Cook at 360ºF (182ºC) for 10 minutes.
5. Flip the salmon steaks halfway through.

6. When cooking is complete, remove from the air fryer oven and divide the salmon steaks among four plates. Serve warm.

Nutrition: Calories: 240 Fat: 10 Fiber: 2 Carbs: 24 Protein: 12

Caesar Shrimp Salad

Preparation time: 10 minutes

Cooking time: 15 minutes

Servings: 4

Ingredients:

- ½ baguette, cut into 1-inch cubes (about 2½ cups)
- 4 tablespoons extra-virgin olive oil, divided
- ¼ teaspoon granulated garlic
- ¼ teaspoon kosher salt
- ¾ cup Caesar dressing, divided
- 2 romaine lettuce hearts, cut in half lengthwise and ends trimmed
- 1 pound (454 g) medium shrimp, peeled and deveined
- 2 ounces (57 g) Parmesan cheese, coarsely grated

Directions:

1. Make the croutons: Put the bread cubes in a medium bowl and drizzle 3 tablespoons of olive oil over top. Season with granulated garlic and salt and toss to coat. Transfer to the air flow racks.
2. Slide the racks into the air fryer oven. Press the Power Button. Cook at 400ºF (205ºC) for 4 minutes.
3. Toss the croutons halfway through the cooking time.

4. When done, remove the air flow racks from the air fryer oven and set aside.
5. Brush 2 tablespoons of Caesar dressing on the cut side of the lettuce. Set aside.
6. Toss the shrimp with the ¼ cup of Caesar dressing in a large bowl until well coated. Set aside.
7. Coat a sheet pan with the remaining 1 tablespoon of olive oil. Arrange the romaine halves on the coated pan, cut side down. Brush the tops with the remaining 2 tablespoons of Caesar dressing.
8. Slide the pan into the air fryer oven. Press the Power Button. Cook at 375ºF (190ºC) for 10 minutes.
9. After 5 minutes, remove from the air fryer oven and flip the romaine halves. Spoon the shrimp around the lettuce. Return to the air fryer oven and continue cooking.
10. When done, remove the sheet pan from the air fryer oven. If they are not quite cooked through, cook for another 1 minute.
11. On each of four plates, put a romaine half. Divide the shrimp among the plates and top with croutons and grated Parmesan cheese. Serve immediately.

Nutrition: Calories: 240 Fat: 10 Fiber: 2 Carbs: 24 Protein: 12

Cajun and Lemon Pepper Cod

Preparation time: 5 minutes

Cooking time: 12 minutes

Servings: 2 cod fillets

Ingredients:
- 1 tablespoon Cajun seasoning
- 1 teaspoon salt
- ½ teaspoon lemon pepper
- ½ teaspoon freshly ground black pepper
- 2 (8-ounce / 227-g) cod fillets, cut to fit into the air flow racks
- Cooking spray
- 2 tablespoons unsalted butter, melted
- 1 lemon, cut into 4 wedges

Directions:
1. Spritz the air flow racks with cooking spray.
2. Thoroughly combine the Cajun seasoning, salt, lemon pepper, and black pepper in a small bowl. Rub this mixture all over the cod fillets until coated.
3. Put the fillets in the air flow racks and brush the melted butter over both sides of each fillet.
4. Slide the racks into the air fryer oven. Press the Power Button. Cook at 360ºF (182ºC) for 12 minutes.
5. Flip the fillets halfway through the cooking time.

6. When cooking is complete, the fish should flake apart with a fork. Remove the fillets from the air fryer oven and serve with fresh lemon wedges.

Nutrition: Calories: 240 Fat: 10 Fiber: 2 Carbs: 24 Protein: 12

Cajun Catfish Cakes with Cheese

Preparation time: 5 minutes
Cooking time: 15 minutes
Servings: 4

Ingredients:

- 2 catfish fillets
- 3 ounces (85 g) butter
- 1 cup shredded Parmesan cheese
- 1 cup shredded Swiss cheese
- ½ cup buttermilk
- 1 teaspoon baking powder
- 1 teaspoon baking soda
- 1 teaspoon Cajun seasoning

Directions:

1. Bring a pot of salted water to a boil. Add the catfish fillets to the boiling water and let them boil for 5 minutes until they become opaque.
2. Remove the fillets from the pot to a mixing bowl and flake them into small pieces with a fork.
3. Add the remaining ingredients to the bowl of fish and stir until well incorporated.
4. Divide the fish mixture into 12 equal portions and shape each portion into a patty. Place the patties in the air flow racks.
5. Slide the racks into the air fryer oven. Press the Power Button. Cook at 380ºF (193ºC) for 15 minutes.

6. Flip the patties halfway through the cooking time.
7. When cooking is complete, the patties should be golden brown and cooked through. Remove from the air fryer oven. Let the patties sit for 5 minutes and serve.

Nutrition: Calories: 240 Fat: 10 Fiber: 2 Carbs: 24 Protein: 12

Cheesy Tuna Patties

Preparation time: 5 minutes

Cooking time: 17 to 18 minutes

Servings: 4

Ingredients:

- Tuna Patties:
- 1 pound (454 g) canned tuna, drained
- 1 egg, whisked
- 2 tablespoons shallots, minced
- 1 garlic clove, minced
- 1 cup grated Romano cheese
- Sea salt and ground black pepper, to taste
- 1 tablespoon sesame oil
- Cheese Sauce:
- 1 tablespoon butter
- 1 cup beer
- 2 tablespoons grated Colby cheese

Directions:

1. Mix the canned tuna, whisked egg, shallots, garlic, cheese, salt, and pepper in a large bowl and stir to incorporate.
2. Divide the tuna mixture into four equal portions and form each portion into a patty with your hands. Refrigerate the patties for 2 hours.
3. When ready, brush both sides of each patty with sesame oil, then place in the air flow racks.
4. Slide the racks into the air fryer oven. Press the Power Button. Cook at 360ºF (182ºC) for 14 minutes.

5. Flip the patties halfway through the cooking time.
6. Meanwhile, melt the butter in a saucepan over medium heat.
7. Pour in the beer and whisk constantly, or until it begins to bubble. Add the grated Colby cheese and mix well. Continue cooking for 3 to 4 minutes, or until the cheese melts. Remove from the heat.
8. When cooking is complete, the patties should be lightly browned and cooked through. Remove the patties from the air fryer oven to a plate. Drizzle them with the cheese sauce and serve immediately.

Nutrition: Calories: 240 Fat: 10 Fiber: 2 Carbs: 24 Protein: 12

Chili Prawns

Preparation time: 10 minutes
Cooking time: 8 minutes
Servings: 2
Ingredients:
- 8 prawns, cleaned
- Salt and black pepper, to taste
- ½ teaspoon ground cayenne pepper
- ½ teaspoon garlic powder
- ½ teaspoon ground cumin
- ½ teaspoon red chili flakes
- Cooking spray

Directions:
1. Spritz the air flow racks with cooking spray.
2. Toss the remaining ingredients in a large bowl until the prawns are well coated.
3. Spread the coated prawns evenly in the air flow racks and spray them with cooking spray.
4. Slide the racks into the air fryer oven. Press the Power Button. Cook at 340ºF (171ºC) for 8 minutes.
5. Flip the prawns halfway through the cooking time.
6. When cooking is complete, the prawns should be pink. Remove the prawns from the air fryer oven to a plate.

Nutrition: Calories: 240 Fat: 10 Fiber: 2 Carbs: 24
Protein: 12

Chili Tuna Casserole

Preparation time: 10 minutes
Cooking time: 16 minutes
Servings: 4

Ingredients:

- ½ tablespoon sesame oil
- $1/_3$ cup yellow onions, chopped
- ½ bell pepper, deveined and chopped
- 2 cups canned tuna, chopped
- Cooking spray
- 5 eggs, beaten
- ½ chili pepper, deveined and finely minced
- 1½ tablespoons sour cream
- $1/_3$ teaspoon dried basil
- $1/_3$ teaspoon dried oregano
- Fine sea salt and ground black pepper, to taste

Directions:

1. Heat the sesame oil in a nonstick skillet over medium heat until it shimmers.
2. Add the onions and bell pepper and sauté for 4 minutes, stirring occasionally, or until tender.
3. Add the canned tuna and keep stirring until the tuna is heated through.
4. Meanwhile, coat a baking dish lightly with cooking spray.
5. Transfer the tuna mixture to the baking dish, along with the beaten eggs, chili pepper, sour

cream, basil, and oregano. Stir to combine well. Season with sea salt and black pepper.

6. Slide the baking dish into the air fryer oven. Press the Power Button. Cook at 325ºF (160ºC) for 12 minutes.

7. When cooking is complete, the eggs should be completely set and the top lightly browned. Remove from the air fryer oven and serve on a plate.

Nutrition: Calories: 240 Fat: 10 Fiber: 2 Carbs: 24 Protein: 12

Coconut Chili Fish Curry

Preparation time: 10 minutes

Cooking time: 22 minutes

Servings: 4

Ingredients:

- 2 tablespoons sunflower oil, divided
- 1 pound (454 g) fish, chopped
- 1 ripe tomato, pureed
- 2 red chilies, chopped
- 1 shallot, minced
- 1 garlic clove, minced
- 1 cup coconut milk
- 1 tablespoon coriander powder
- 1 teaspoon red curry paste
- ½ teaspoon fenugreek seeds
- Salt and white pepper, to taste

Directions:

1. Coat the air flow racks with 1 tablespoon of sunflower oil. Place the fish in the air flow racks.
2. Slide the racks into the air fryer oven. Press the Power Button. Cook at 380ºF (193ºC) for 10 minutes.
3. Flip the fish halfway through the cooking time.
4. When cooking is complete, transfer the cooked fish to a baking pan greased with the remaining 1 tablespoon of sunflower oil. Stir in the remaining ingredients.

5. Slide the pan into the air fryer oven. Press the Power Button. Cook at 350ºF (180ºC) for 12 minutes.
6. When cooking is complete, they should be heated through. Cool for 5 to 8 minutes before serving.

Nutrition: Calories: 240 Fat: 10 Fiber: 2 Carbs: 24 Protein: 12

SIDES

Cajun Zucchini Chips

Preparation Time: 5 Minutes

Cooking Time: 16 Minutes

Servings: 4

Ingredients:
- Two large zucchinis, cut into 1/8-inch-thick slices
- Two teaspoons Cajun seasoning
- Cooking spray

Directions:
1. Preheat the air fryer oven to 370ºF (188ºC).
2. Spray the air fryer basket lightly with cooking spray.
3. Put the zucchini slices in a medium bowl and spray them generously with cooking spray.
4. Sprinkle the Cajun seasoning over the zucchini and stir to make sure they are evenly coated with oil and seasoning.
5. Position the slices in a single layer in the air fryer basket, making sure not to overcrowd.
6. Place the air fryer basket onto the baking pan.
7. Slide into Rack Position 2
8. Select Air Fry and set the time to 8 minutes.
9. Flip the slices over and air fry for an additional 7 to 8 minutes, or until they are as crunchy and brown as you prefer.
10.   Serve immediately.

Nutrition: Calories: 367 Fat: 28g Carbohydrates: 5g Protein: 4g

Cheesy Apple Roll-Ups

Preparation Time: 5 Minutes
Cooking Time: 5 Minutes
Servings: 8

Ingredients:

- Eight slices whole wheat sandwich bread
- 4 ounces (113 g) Colby Jack cheese, grated
- ½ small apple, chopped
- Two tablespoons butter, melted

Directions:

1. Preheat the air fryer oven to 390ºF (199ºC).
2. Take away the crusts from the bread and flatten the slices with a rolling pin. Don't be gentle. Press hard so that the bread will be fragile.
3. Top bread slices with cheese and chopped apple, dividing the ingredients evenly.
4. Roll up each slice tightly and secure each with one or two toothpicks.
5. Brush outside of rolls with melted butter. Place them in the air fryer basket.
6. Place the air fryer basket onto the baking pan.
7. Slide into Rack Position 2, select Air Fry, and set time to 5 minutes. You may also wait until the outside is crisp and nicely browned.
8. Serve hot.

Nutrition: Calories: 147 Fat: 9.5g Carbohydrates: 13.8g Sugar: 2.1g Protein: 1.9g Sodium: 62mg

Cheesy Jalapeño Poppers

Preparation Time: 5 Minutes

Cooking Time: 10 Minutes

Servings: 4

Ingredients:
- Eight jalapeño peppers
- ½ cup whipped cream cheese
- ¼ cup shredded Cheddar cheese

Directions:
1. Preheat the air fryer oven to 360ºF (182ºC).
2. Practice a paring knife to carefully cut off the jalapeño tops, then scoop out the ribs and seeds. Set aside.
3. In a medium bowl, combine the whipped cream cheese and shredded Cheddar cheese. Place the mixture in a sealable plastic bag, and using a pair of scissors, cut off one corner from the bag. Gently squeeze some cream cheese mixture into each pepper until almost full.
4. Place a piece of parchment paper on the bottom of the air fryer basket and place the poppers on top, distributing evenly.
5. Place the air fryer basket onto the baking pan.
6. Slide into Rack Position 2, select Air Fry, and set time to 10 minutes.
7. Allow the poppers to cool for 5 to 10 minutes before serving.

Nutrition: Calories: 456 Fat: 60g Carbohydrates: 7g
Protein: 15g

Cheesy Steak Fries

Preparation Time: 5 Minutes
Cooking Time: 20 Minutes
Servings: 5

Ingredients:

- 1 (28-ounce / 794-g) bag frozen steak fries
- Cooking spray
- ½ cup beef gravy
- 1 cup shredded Mozzarella cheese
- Two scallions, green parts only, chopped

Directions:

1. Preheat the air fryer oven to 400°F (204°C).
2. Place the frozen steak fries in the air fryer basket.
3. Place the air fryer basket onto the baking pan.
4. Slide into Rack Position 2, select Air Fry, and set time to 10 minutes.
5. Shake the basket and spritz the fries with cooking spray. Sprinkle with salt and pepper. Air fry for an additional 8 minutes.
6. Pour the beef gravy into a medium, microwave-safe bowl—microwave for 30 seconds, or until the sauce is warm.
7. Sprinkle the fries with the cheese. Air fry for an additional 2 minutes until the cheese is melted.
8. Transfer the fries to a serving dish. Drizzle the fries with gravy and sprinkle the scallions on top for a green garnish. Serve warm.

Nutrition: Calories 1536 Fat 123.7 g Protein 103.4 g

Crispy Breaded Beef Cubes

Preparation Time: 10 Minutes

Cooking Time: 8 Minutes

Servings: 4

Ingredients:

- 1-pound (454 g) sirloin tip, cut into 1-inch cubes
- 1 cup cheese pasta sauce
- 1½ cups soft bread crumbs
- Two tablespoons olive oil
- ½ teaspoon dried marjoram

Directions:

1. Preheat the air fryer oven to 360°F (182°C).
2. In a medium container, toss the beef with the pasta sauce to coat.
3. In a shallow bowl, blend the bread crumbs, oil, and marjoram, and stir completely. Put the beef cubes, one at a time, into the bread crumb mixture to coat methodically. Transfer the beef to the air fryer basket.
4. Place the air fryer basket onto the baking pan.
5. Slide into Rack Position 2, select Air Fry, set time to 8 minutes, or until the beef is at least 145°F (63°C), and the outside is crisp and brown. Shake the basket once during cooking time.
6. Serve hot.

Nutrition: Calories: 262 kcal Total Fat: 9.4g Carbs: 8.2g Protein: 16.2g

Crispy Cajun Dill Pickle Chips

Preparation Time: 5 Minutes
Cooking Time: 5 Minutes
Servings: 16

Ingredients:

- ¼ cup all-purpose flour
- ½ cup panko bread crumbs
- One large egg, beaten
- Two teaspoons Cajun seasoning
- Two large dill pickles, sliced into eight rounds each

Directions:

1. Preheat the air fryer oven to 390ºF (199ºC).
2. Place the all-purpose flour, panko bread crumbs, and egg into three separate shallow bowls, then stir the Cajun seasoning into the flour.
3. Dredge each pickle chip in the flour mixture, then the egg, and finally the bread crumbs. Shake off any excess, then place each coated pickle chip on a plate.
4. Spritz the air fryer basket by means of cooking spray, then place the pickle chips in the basket.
5. Place the air fryer basket onto the baking pan.
6. Slide into Rack Position 2, select Air Fry, set time to 5 minutes, or wait until crispy and golden brown.

7. Remove the chips and allow to slightly cool on a wire rack before serving.

Nutrition: Calories: 367 Fat: 28g Carbohydrates: 5g Protein: 4g

Jicama Fries

Preparation Time: 5 Minutes
Cooking Time: 30 Minutes
Servings: 4
Ingredients:
- One small jicama, peeled.
- ¼ tsp. onion powder.
- ¾tsp. chili powder
- ¼ tsp. ground black pepper
- ¼ tsp. garlic powder.

Directions:
1. Cut jicama into matchstick-sized pieces.
2. Place pieces into a small bowl and sprinkle with remaining ingredients. Place the fries into the air fryer basket
3. Adjust the temperature to 350 Degrees F and set the timer for 20 minutes. Toss the basket two- or three times during cooking. Serve warm.

Nutrition: Calories: 37 Protein: 0.8g Fiber: 4.7g Fat: 0.1g Carbs: 8.7g

Kale Chips

Preparation Time: 5 Minutes
Cooking Time: 10 Minutes
Servings: 4
Ingredients:
- 4 cups stemmed kale
- ½ tsp. salt
- 2 tsp. avocado oil

Directions:
1. Take a large bowl, toss the kale in avocado oil and sprinkle with salt. Place into the air fryer basket.
2. Adjust the temperature to 400 Degrees F and set the timer for 5 minutes. Kale will be crispy when done. Serve immediately.

Nutrition: Calories: 25 Protein: 0.5g Fiber: 0.4g Fat: 2.2g Carbs: 1.1g

Coriander Artichokes

Preparation Time: 5 Minutes
Cooking Time: 20 Minutes
Servings: 4

Ingredients:
- 12 oz. artichoke hearts
- 1 tbsp. lemon juice
- 1 tsp. coriander, ground
- ½ tsp. cumin seeds
- ½ tsp. olive oil

Directions:
1. Mix all the ingredients, toss.
2. Introduce the pan in the fryer and cook at 370°F for 15 minutes
3. Divide the mix between plates and serve as a side dish.

Nutrition: Calories: 200 Fat: 7g Fiber: 2g Carbs: 5g Protein: 8g

Spinach and Artichokes Sauté

Preparation Time: 5 Minutes
Cooking Time: 20 Minutes
Servings: 4

Ingredients:

- 10 oz. artichoke hearts; halved
- 2 cups baby spinach
- Three garlic cloves
- ¼ cup veggie stock
- 2 tsp. lime juice
- Salt and black pepper to taste.

Directions:

1. Mix all the ingredients, toss, introduce in the fryer and cook at 370°F for 15 minutes
2. Divide between plates and serve.

Nutrition: Calories: 209 Fat: 6g Fiber: 2g Carbs: 4g Protein: 8g

DESSERTS

Zucchini Bread

Preparation time: 10 minutes
Cooking time: 40 minutes
Servings: 12

Ingredients:

- 2 cups coconut flour
- 2 teaspoons baking powder
- ¾ cup erythritol
- ½ cup coconut oil, melted
- 1 teaspoon apple cider vinegar
- 1 teaspoon vanilla extract
- 3 eggs, beaten
- 1 zucchini, grated
- 1 teaspoon ground cinnamon

Directions:

1. In the mixing bowl, mix coconut flour with baking powder, erythritol, coconut oil, apple cider vinegar, vanilla extract, eggs, zucchini, and ground cinnamon.
2. Transfer the mixture in the air fryer basket and flatten it in the shape of the bread.
3. Cook the bread at 350F (180ºC) for 40 minutes.

Nutrition: Calories: 179 Fat: 12g Protein: 4g Carbs: 15g Net carbs: 7g Fiber: 8g

Creamy Vanilla Scones

Preparation time: 20 minutes

Cooking time: 10 minutes

Servings: 6

Ingredients:

- 4 oz coconut flour
- ½ teaspoon baking powder
- 1 teaspoon apple cider vinegar
- 2 teaspoons mascarpone
- ¼ cup heavy cream
- 1 teaspoon vanilla extract
- 1 tablespoon erythritol
- Cooking spray

Directions:

1. In the mixing bowl, mix coconut flour with baking powder, apple cider vinegar, mascarpone, heavy cream, vanilla extract, and erythritol.
2. Knead the dough and cut into scones.
3. Then put them in the air fryer basket and sprinkle with cooking spray.
4. Cook the vanilla scones at 365F (185ºC) for 10 minutes.

Nutrition: Calories: 104 Fat: 4g Protein: 3g Carbs: 14g Net carbs: 6g Fiber: 8g

Homemade Mint Pie

Preparation time: 15 minutes
Cooking time: 25 minutes
Servings: 2

Ingredients:

- 1 tablespoon instant coffee
- 2 tablespoons almond butter, softened
- 2 tablespoons erythritol
- 1 teaspoon dried mint
- 3 eggs, beaten
- 1 teaspoon spearmint, dried
- 4 teaspoons coconut flour
- Cooking spray

Directions:

1. Spray the air fryer basket with cooking spray.
2. Then mix all ingredients in the mixer bowl.
3. When you get a smooth mixture, transfer it in the air fryer basket. Flatten it gently.
4. Cook the pie at 365F (185ºC) for 25 minutes.

Nutrition: Calories: 313 Fat: 19g Protein: 16g Carbs: 20g Net carbs: 8g Fiber: 12g

Cheese Keto Balls

Preparation time: 15 minutes

Cooking time: 4 minutes

Servings: 10

Ingredients:

- 2 eggs, beaten
- 1 teaspoon coconut oil, melted
- 9 oz coconut flour
- 5 oz provolone cheese, shredded
- 2 tablespoons erythritol
- 1 teaspoon baking powder
- ¼ teaspoon ground coriander
- Cooking spray

Directions:

1. Mix eggs with coconut oil, coconut flour, Provolone cheese, erythritol, baking powder, and ground cinnamon.
2. Make the balls and put them in the air fryer basket.
3. Sprinkle the balls with cooking spray and cook at 400F (205ºC) for 4 minutes.

Nutrition: Calories: 176 Fat: 7g Protein: 8g Carbs: 19g Net carbs: 8g Fiber: 11g

Pecan Butter Cookie

Preparation time: 5 minutes
Cooking time: 24 minutes
Servings: 12 cookies

Ingredients:

- 1 cup chopped pecans
- ½ cup salted butter, melted
- ½ cup coconut flour
- ¾ cup erythritol, divided
- 1 teaspoon vanilla extract

Directions:

1. In a food processor, blend together pecans, butter, flour, ½ cup erythritol, and vanilla 1 minute until a dough form.
2. Form dough into twelve individual cookie balls, about 1 tablespoon each.
3. Cut three pieces of parchment to fit air fryer basket. Place four cookies on each ungreased parchment and place one piece parchment with cookies into air fryer basket. Adjust air fryer temperature to 325°F (163ºC) and set the timer for 8 minutes. Repeat cooking with remaining batches.
4. When the timer goes off, allow cookies to cool 5 minutes on a large serving plate until cool enough to handle. While still warm, dust cookies with

remaining erythritol. Allow to cool completely, about 15 minutes, before serving.

Nutrition: Calories: 151 Fat: 14g Protein: 2g Carbs: 13g Net carbs: 10g Fiber: 3g

Golden Doughnut Holes

Preparation time: 10 minutes

Cooking time: 6 minutes

Servings: 20 doughnut holes

Ingredients:

- 1 cup blanched finely ground almond flour
- ½ cup low-carb vanilla protein powder
- ½ cup granular erythritol
- ¼ cup unsweetened cocoa powder
- ½ teaspoon baking powder
- 2 large eggs, whisked
- ½ teaspoon vanilla extract

Directions:

1. Mix all ingredients in a large bowl until a soft dough form. Separate and roll dough into twenty balls, about 2 tablespoons each.
2. Cut a piece of parchment to fit your air fryer basket. Working in batches if needed, place doughnut holes into air fryer basket on ungreased parchment. Adjust the temperature to 380°F (193ºC) and set the timer for 6 minutes, flipping doughnut holes halfway through cooking. Doughnut holes will be golden and firm when done. Let cool completely before serving, about 10 minutes.

Nutrition: Calories: 103 Fat: 7g Protein: 8g Carbs: 13g Net carbs: 11g Fiber: 2g

Chocolate Chips Soufflés

Preparation time: 5 minutes
Cooking time: 15 minutes
Servings: 2

Ingredients:

- 2 large eggs, whites and yolks separated
- 1 teaspoon vanilla extract
- 2 ounces (57 g) low-carb chocolate chips
- 2 teaspoons coconut oil, melted

Directions:

1. In a medium bowl, beat egg whites until stiff peaks form, about 2 minutes. Set aside. In a separate medium bowl, whisk egg yolks and vanilla together. Set aside.
2. In a separate medium microwave-safe bowl, place chocolate chips and drizzle with coconut oil. Microwave on high 20 seconds, then stir and continue cooking in 10-second increments until melted, being careful not to overheat chocolate. Let cool 1 minute.
3. Slowly pour melted chocolate into egg yolks and whisk until smooth. Then, slowly begin adding egg white mixture to chocolate mixture, about ¼ cup at a time, folding in gently.
4. Pour mixture into two 4-inch ramekins greased with cooking spray. Place ramekins into air fryer basket. Adjust the temperature to 400°F (205°C)

and set the timer for 15 minutes. Soufflés will puff up while cooking and deflate a little once cooled. The center will be set when done. Let cool 10 minutes, then serve warm.

Nutrition: Calories: 217 Fat: 18g Protein: 8g Carbs: 19g Net carbs: 11g Fiber: 8g

Creamy Strawberry Pecan Pie

Preparation time: 15 minutes

Cooking time: 10 minutes

Servings: 6

Ingredients:

- 1½ cups whole shelled pecans
- 1 tablespoon unsalted butter, softened
- 1 cup heavy whipping cream
- 12 medium fresh strawberries, hulled
- 2 tablespoons sour cream

Directions:

1. Place pecans and butter into a food processor and pulse ten times until a dough form. Press dough into the bottom of an ungreased 6-inch round nonstick baking dish.
2. Place dish into air fryer basket. Adjust the temperature to 320°F (160°C) and set the timer for 10 minutes. Crust will be firm and golden when done. Let cool 20 minutes.
3. In a large bowl, whisk cream until fluffy and doubled in size, about 2 minutes.
4. In a separate large bowl, mash strawberries until mostly liquid. Fold strawberries and sour cream into whipped cream.
5. Spoon mixture into cooled crust, cover, and place into refrigerator for at least 30 minutes to set. Serve chilled.

Nutrition: Calories: 340 Fat: 33g Protein: 3g Carbs: 7g Net carbs: 4g Fiber: 3g

Chocolate Chip Cookie Cake

Preparation time: 5 minutes

Cooking time: 15 minutes

Servings: 8

Ingredients:

- 4 tablespoons salted butter, melted
- $1/_3$ cup granular brown erythritol
- 1 large egg
- ½ teaspoon vanilla extract
- 1 cup blanched finely ground almond flour
- ½ teaspoon baking powder
- ¼ cup low-carb chocolate chips

Directions:

1. In a large bowl, whisk together butter, erythritol, egg, and vanilla. Add flour and baking powder, and stir until combined.
2. Fold in chocolate chips, then spoon batter into an ungreased 6-inch round nonstick baking dish.
3. Place dish into air fryer basket. Adjust the temperature to 300°F (150ºC) and set the timer for 15 minutes. When edges are browned, cookie cake will be done.
4. Slice and serve warm.

Nutrition: Calories: 170 Fat: 16g Protein: 4g Carbs: 15g Net carbs: 11g Fiber: 4g

Homemade Pretzels

Preparation time: 10 minutes

Cooking time: 10 minutes

Servings: 6

Ingredients:

- 1½ cups shredded Mozzarella cheese
- 1 cup blanched finely ground almond flour
- 2 tablespoons salted butter, melted, divided
- ¼ cup granular erythritol, divided
- 1 teaspoon ground cinnamon

Directions:

1. Place Mozzarella, flour, 1 tablespoon butter, and 2 tablespoons erythritol in a large microwave-safe bowl. Microwave on high 45 seconds, then stir with a fork until a smooth dough ball form.
2. Separate dough into six equal sections. Gently roll each section into a 12 -inch rope, then fold into a pretzel shape.
3. Place pretzels into ungreased air fryer basket. Adjust the temperature to 370°F (188ºC) and set the timer for 8 minutes, turning pretzels halfway through cooking.
4. In a small bowl, combine remaining butter, remaining erythritol, and cinnamon. Brush ½ mixture on both sides of pretzels.
5. Place pretzels back into air fryer and cook an additional 2 minutes at 370°F (188ºC).

6. Transfer pretzels to a large plate. Brush on both sides with remaining butter mixture, then let cool 5 minutes before serving.

Nutrition: Calories: 223 Fat: 19g Protein: 11g Carbs: 13g Net carbs: 11g Fiber: 2g

CONCLUSION

Hopefully, after going through this book and trying out a couple of recipes, you will get to understand the flexibility and utility of the air fryers. It is undoubtedly a multipurpose kitchen appliance that is highly recommended to everybody. It presents one with a palatable atmosphere to enjoy fried foods that are not only delicious but healthy, cheaper, and more convenient. The use of this kitchen appliance ensures that the making of some of your favorite snacks and meals will be carried out in a stress-free manner without hassling around, which invariably legitimizes its worth and gives you value for your money.

This book will be your all-time guide to understanding the basics of the air fryer because, with all the recipes stated in the book, it rests assured that it will be something that you and the rest of the people around the world will enjoy for the rest of your lives. Also, after going completely with this book, you will be able to prepare delicious and flavorsome meals that will be easy to carry out but tasty and healthy.

However, you should never limit yourself to the recipes solely mentioned in this cookbook, go on and try new things! Explore new recipes! Experiment with different ingredients, seasonings, and various methods! Create some new recipes and keep your mind open. By so doing, you will be able to get the best out of your air fryer.

Throughout this book, we have learned a lot about owning and using an air fryer. We can confidently say that the air fryer is one of the best inventions of kitchen appliances.

Healthy food should not be a fad or an impossibility to choose; it should be part of everyone's life. Of course, this does not mean that you must give up enjoying the kitchen; neither of the many dishes can be prepared healthily. To get it, certain appliances can help you and a lot: for example, an air fryer.

In our earlier pages, you could see that you will cook different foods with an air fryer in a similar way as a traditional one would. But thanks to its special operation, you can do it without using a single drop of oil. In this way, you can prepare exquisite dishes without added fats and with a considerably lower caloric intake.

Now you know some of the many functions and recipes of an air fryer. We hope that this eBook has helped you discover some interesting features.

Having an air fryer is a great option. You can enjoy a healthier meal and save a good part of the oil expense, all without giving up enjoyable, fried foods

Please enjoy the different recipes that we have listed for you in this cookbook.

In a nutshell, if you found this book helpful, please kindly take the time to leave an honest opinion on Amazon. Your feedback will be greatly appreciated. Thank you, and best wishes to you!